To:_____

From:_____

Date:_____

Simple Wisdom of Living

Created by Marge McDonald and Richard J. Lenz

Illustrations by Addison

Longstreet
Atlanta, Georgia

Published by LONGSTREET PRESS, INC.
A subsidiary of Cox Newspapers
A division of Cox Enterprises, Inc.
2140 Newmarket Parkway, Suite 122
Atlanta, Georgia 30309

Copyright © 1999 by McDonald & Lenz, Inc.
Design by Lenz Design & Communications, Inc., Decatur, GA

Printed in the United States of America, 1st printing, 1999.

Library of Congress Card Catalog Number: 98-89175
ISBN: 1-56352-560-7

*In many cases we've taken a little liberty with poets' and writers' lines to fit this book
but credited them where we knew who wrote the basic words. We sincerely hope
in their wisdom they forgive us.*

To **quote** copiously and well, requires taste, judgement, and erudition, a feeling for the beautiful, an appreciation of the noble, and a sense of the profound.
—*C. Nestell Boves*

Any idiot can face a crisis: It is this day-to-day living that wears you out.
—*Anton Chekov*

After the game's over
the king and pawn go in the same box.
—*Italian saying*

A well-written life is almost as rare as a well-spent one.
—*Thomas Carlyle*

After a fierce thunderstorm,
the weather takes a pledge and signs it with a rainbow.
—*Thomas Aldrich*

A meowing cat can't catch mice.
—*Yiddish saying*

A smart man makes no minor blunders.
—*Johann von Goethe*

A sense of humor keen enough to show a man
his own absurdities will keep him from all sins,
save those that are worth committing.
—*Samuel Butler*

All sins cast long shadows.
—*Irish saying*

A good person attracts good people, and knows how to keep them as friends.
—*Johann von Goethe*

A good name is better than a girdle of gold.
—*French saying*

Always do right. This will gratify some people and astonish the rest.
—*Mark Twain*

A good folly is worth whatever we pay for it.
—*George Ade*

A picture is a poem without words.
—*Horace*

Act quickly, think slowly.
—*Roman proverb*

Body:

A thing of shreds
and patches, borrowed unequally
from good and bad ancestors
and a misfit from the start.
—*Ralph Waldo Emerson*

Better the devil you know than the devil you don't.
—*Yiddish proverb*

Believe me, everything is funny,
as long as it's happening to somebody else.
—*Will Rogers*

Beware of little expenses:
a small leak will sink a great ship.
—*Benjamin Franklin*

Be intent upon the perfection of today.
—*William Law*

Books are good in their own way,
but they are a mighty bloodless substitute
for living.
—*Robert Louis Stevenson*

By wisdom, wealth is won.
—*Bayard Taylor*

Beware, beware; he'll cheat without scruple, who can cheat without fear.
—*Benjamin Franklin*

Better a witty fool than a foolish wit.
—*William Shakespeare*

Beware lest you lose the substance by grasping at the shadow.
—*Aesop*

Be as great in the act as you are in the thought!
—*William Shakespeare*

Best way to keep one's word is not to give it.
—*Napoleon Bonaparte*

Big shots are only little shots who keep shooting.
—*Christopher Morley*

Be slow in choosing a friend, slower in changing.
—*Benjamin Franklin*

A rock pile **Ceases** to be a rock pile the moment a single man contemplates it, bearing within him the image of a cathedral.

—*Antoine de Saint-Exupery*

Content makes poor men rich; discontent makes rich men poor.
—*Samuel Johnson*

Cheaply bought, dear in the end.
—*Spanish saying*

Curiosity is the lust of the mind.
—*Thomas Hobbes*

Cowardice is simply a lack of the ability
to suspend the functioning of the imagination.
—*Ernest Hemingway*

Chance is powerful, in the pool
where you least expect it will be the fish.
—*Ovid*

Courage is a quality necessary for maintaining virtue
and it is always respected,
even when it is associated with vice.
—*Samuel Johnson*

Clever men are impressed by their differences
from their fellows.
Wise men are conscious of their resemblance to them.
—*Richard H. Tawney*

Character building begins in infancy, and continues until death.
—*Eleanor Roosevelt*

Curiosity is one of the permanent
and certain characteristics of a vigorous mind.
—*Samuel Johnson*

Comedy is just a funny way of being serious.
—*Peter Ustinov*

Caricature: putting the face of a joke
upon the body of a truth.
—*Joseph Conrad*

Chop your own wood and it will warm you twice!
—*Benjamin Franklin*

Don't let your will roar when your power only whispers.
—*Thomas Fuller*

Doing easily what others find difficult is talent;
doing what is impossible for the talented is genius.
—*Henri Frédéric Amiel*

Don't take a fence down
unless you know why it was put up.
—*Robert Frost*

Dwell on your misfortunes
and the greater is their power to harm.
—*Voltaire*

Defer not till tomorrow to be wise.
—*William Congreve*

Dealing with the negatives that pepper life
is the first step in eliminating them.
—*Anonymous*

Don't put too fine a pen to your wit for fear it might get blunted.
—*Miguel de Cervantes*

Drawing on my fine command of language,
I said nothing.
—*Robert Benchley*

Determine never to be idle.
No person will have occasion
to complain of the want of time
who never loses any.
—*Thomas Jefferson*

Drink in life to its fullest,
and drain the cup without concern.
—*Italian saying*

Don't take yourself too seriously
or you'll look ridiculous.
—*Anonymous*

Daily existence is a strange bargain.
Life's only true happiness comes
from squandering ourselves for a purpose.
—*William Cowper*

Every man's life
is a fairy tale written
by God's fingers.
—*Hans Christian Anderson*

Fame due to the achievements of the mind never perishes.
—*Propertius*

Fiction reveals truth that reality obscures.
—*Jessamyn West*

Foolish men and the dead alone never change their opinions.
—*James Russell Lowell*

Few people are as obnoxious as a learned n'er-do-well.
—*Scottish saying*

Fortune brings in some boats that are not steered.
—*William Shakespeare*

From a fallen tree, many make kindling.
—*Spanish proverb*

Faith is believing what you know ain't so.
—*Mark Twain*

Fortune favors the bold.
—*Yonge*

For extremes meet, and there is no better example
than the haughtiness of humility.
—*Ralph Waldo Emerson*

Flesh endures the storms of the present alone,
the mind, those of the past and present.
—*Epictetus*

Fame has often created something from nothing.
—*Thomas Fuller*

Failure is not our only punishment for laziness,
there is also the success of others.
—*Jules Renard*

Four be the things I'd have been better without:
love, curiosity, freckles and doubt.
—*Dorothy Parker*

Fearful unbelief is unbelief in yourself.
—*Thomas Carlyle*

Great minds, like most everything else, need to be closed down every once in awhile for repairs.

—*Anonymous*

Please wake up at 10th St. station

Getting others to come to our way of thinking,
we must go over to theirs for it's necessary
to follow before we can lead.
—*William Hazlitt*

Genius has limits; stupidity has none; that is the difference.
—*Irish saying*

Good breeding is a union of kindness and independence.
—*Ralph Waldo Emerson*

Genius is to humor what the whole is in proportion to its parts.
—*Jean de La Bruyére*

Great pleasure is gained from useless knowledge.
—*Bertrand Russell*

Growing up is a terribly hard thing to do.
It is much easier to skip it
and go from one childhood to the next.
—*F. Scott Fitzgerald*

Genius must be born and never can be taught.
—*John Dryden*

Great laws of culture let each of us
become all that we were created capable of being.
—*Thomas Carlyle*

Genius is one percent inspiration
and ninety-nine percent perspiration.
—*Thomas Edison*

Gossip is as smoke from the pipe of those who diffuse it;
it proves nothing but the bad taste of the smoker.
—*George Eliot*

Genius may have its limitations,
but stupidity is not thus handicapped.
—*Elbert Hubbard*

Great talkers should be cropp'd, for they have no need of ears.
—*Benjamin Franklin*

Heredity:

An omnibus in which
all our ancestors ride,
and every now and then
one of them puts his head
out and embarrasses us.
—*Oliver Wendell Holmes*

He is a fool who leaves things close at hand to follow a dream out of reach.
—*Plutarch*

How unhappy he is who cannot forgive himself.
—*Publilius Syrus*

Health is worth more than brilliance.
—*Thomas Jefferson*

Humor has justly been regarded as the finest perfection of poetic genius.
—*Thomas Carlyle*

He who knows others is wise; he who knows himself is enlightened.
—*Chinese saying*

Hands that follow intellect can achieve art.
—*Michaelangelo*

Having a good mind is not enough. The main thing is to use it well.
—*Rene Descartes*

He who lives without folly is not so wise as he thinks.
—*Francois Duc de La Rochefoucauld*

Have many acquaintances, but choose just a few friends.
—*Spanish saying*

Health and cheerfulness mutually beget each other.
—*Joseph Addison*

Happiest of conversations is the one of which
nothing is distinctly remembered
but a general effect of pleasing impression.
—*Samuel Johnson*

Happy are you, as if every day
you have picked up a horseshoe.
—*Henry Wadsworth Longfellow*

Habit is habit, and not to be thrown out
but coaxed downstairs a step at a time.
—*Mark Twain*

It is more

from carelessness about the truth than from intentional lying that there is so much falsehood in the world.

—*Samuel Johnson*

I like the dreams of the future better than the history of the past.
—*Thomas Jefferson*

I haven't heard of anybody
who wants to stop living on account of the cost.
—*Abe Martin*

If you won't be better tomorrow
than you were today, you don't need tomorrow.
—*Jewish saying*

I've never had pity for conceited people
because I'm sure they carry their comfort about with them.
—*George Eliot*

If you want people to think well of you,
do not speak well of yourself.
—*Blaise Pascal*

I never forgive, but I always forget.
—*Arthur J. Balfour*

Improvement makes straight roads
but the crooked roads without improvement
are the roads of genius.
—*William Blake*

It is good to be thrifty,
just don't collect a hoard of regrets.
—*French saying*

It is impossible to live pleasurably without living wisely, well,
and justly, and impossible to live wisely,
well, and justly without living pleasurably.
—*Epictetus*

It may not be natural for man to walk on two legs,
but it was a noble invention.
—*Georg C. Lichtenberg*

It's the mind that makes the body rich.
—*William Shakespeare*

It appears to me that almost any man may,
like the spider, spin from his inwards
his own citadel.
—*John Keats*

Illusion is the first of all pleasures.
—*Voltaire*

Intellect is invisible to the man who has none.
—*Arthur Schopenhauer*

It is indeed desirable to be well descended,
but the glory belongs to our ancestors.
—*Plutarch*

If you are all wrapped up in yourself
you are overdressed!
—*Proverbs*

If ill luck falls asleep, let nobody wake her.
—*Spanish saying*

I like Wagner's music better
than any other.
It is so loud that one is able to talk the whole time
without other people hearing what one says.
That is a great advantage.
—*Oscar Wilde*

Imagination rules the world.
—*Napoleon Bonaparte*

It pays a whole lot better
to get even with your friends
instead of your enemies.
—*Irish saying*

It must be great t' be rich an' let
th' other feller keep up appearances.
—*Abe Martin*

If there were not bad people
there would be no good lawyers.
—*Charles Dickens*

The **Job** of
intellectuals is to come up
with ideas, and all we've
been producing is footnotes.
—*Theodore H. White*

The **Keenest**
sorrow is to recognize
ourselves as the sole
cause of all
our adversities.
—*Sophocles*

Let us go singing far as we go; the road will be less tedious.
—*Virgil*

Like all weak men he laid exaggerated stress
on not changing anyone's mind.
—*Somerset Maugham*

Liberty means responsibility and that's why many dread it.
—*George Bernard Shaw*

Life is not life at all without delight.
—*Coventry Patmore*

Life is painting a picture, not doing a sum.
—*Oliver Wendall Holmes, Jr.*

Life is a handful of one-act plays,
pretending to be an opera.
—*Anonymous*

Life is ours to be spent, not to be saved.
—*D. H. Lawrence*

Life does not move so fast
that there is not enough time for courtesy.
—*Ralph Waldo Emerson*

Luck comes to all who work at making it happen.
—*Old wives tale*

Life is the art of drawing sufficient conclusions
from insufficient premises.
—*Samuel Butler*

Laughter is about as close to the grace of God as anything gets.
—*Anonymous*

Little is needed to make a happy life.
—*Marcus Aurelius*

Letter-writing and reading are the only devices
for combining solitude
with good company.
—*Lord Byron*

 **Man** is the only animal that blushes or needs to.
—*Mark Twain*

Meddling with another man's folly
is always thankless work.
—*Rudyard Kipling*

Money is your sixth sense without which
you cannot make complete use of the other five.
—*Somerset Maugham*

Moderation is the silken string
running through the pearl-chain of all virtues.
—*Thomas Fuller*

Mind unemployed is mind unenjoyed.
—*Nestell Bovee*

Measure your mind's height by the shade it casts.
—*Robert Browning*

Mean tempers and fretful dispositions
make any state of life unhappy.
—*Cicero*

My visitors, if they cannot see the clock,
should find the time in my face.
—*Ralph Waldo Emerson*

Most of the trouble in the world is caused
by people wanting to be important.
—*T. S. Eliot*

Man lives *by* habits, indeed,
but what he lives *for* is thrills and excitements.
—*William James*

My way of joking is to tell the truth.
It's the funniest joke in the world.
—*George Bernard Shaw*

Most demoralizin' thing in th' world is a rich loafer.
—*Abe Martin*

Mistake, error, is the discipline through which we advance.
—*Channing*

No man will be found
in whose mind airy notions
do not sometimes tyrannize,
and force him to hope or fear
beyond the limits of sober
probability.
—*Samuel Johnson*

Never doubt that a small group of thoughtful,
committed, ordinary folks can change the world;
indeed it's the only thing that ever has.
—*John Adams*

Nothing is so firmly believed as what we least know.
—*Michel Montaigne*

No place affords a more striking conviction
of the vanity of human hopes than a public library.
—*Samuel Johnson*

Name the greatest of all inventors: Accident.
—*Mark Twain*

No bird soars too high if he soars with his own wings.
—*William Blake*

Nature never makes any blunders;
when she makes a fool she means it.
—*Josh Billings*

No man can live without folly so long as he pursues love.
—*Jean-Louis de Balzac*

No man who has once heartily and wholly laughed
can be altogether irreclaimably bad.
—*Thomas Carlyle*

No one is free who is not master of themselves.
—*Epictetus*

Next to a fourteen-year-old boy
ther hain't nothin' as worthless
as th' average opinion.
—*Abe Martin*

Nothing is more terrible than active ignorance.
—*Johann Goethe*

Nature never stands still, no souls neither;
they forever go up or go down.
—*Julia C. R. Dorr*

Oh! For a life
of sensations rather
than of thoughts.
—*John Keats*

Old-fashioned advice is usually great advice.
—*Anonymous*

One of the great pleasures in life
is doing what people say you cannot do.
—*Walter Bagehot*

One way to get rid of temptation is to yield to it.
—*Oscar Wilde*

One of the marks of mediocrity of understanding
is to be always telling jokes and stories.
—*French saying*

One man who has a mind and knows
it can always beat ten men
who haven't one and don't know it.
—*George Bernard Shaw*

Opinion is ultimately determined by feelings, and not by intellect.
—*Herbert Spencer*

One thing I know, those amongst us
who will be really happy are those who have sought
and have found how to serve.
—*Albert Schweitzer*

One man in his time plays many parts.
—*William Shakespeare*

Out of intense complexities, intense simplicities emerge.
—*Winston Churchill*

Offer compassion to the deserters of the family
and let them spread their wings.
Like Canada geese they'll return.
—*Anonymous*

Only so much do I know, as I have lived.
—*Ralph Waldo Emerson*

O precious evenings! All too swiftly you have sped!
—*Henry Wadsworth Longfellow*

 **People** only see what they are prepared to see.

—*Ralph Waldo Emerson*

**The wisdom of the wise,
and the experience of ages,
may be preserved by**
Quotations.
—*Issac D'Israeli*

Results!

Why, man, I have gotten
results. I know several
thousand things that
won't work.

—*Thomas A. Edison*

Remember, judge a man by his questions
rather than his answers.
—*Thomas A. Edison*

Reading is to the mind what exercise is to the body.
—*Joseph Addison*

Reason respects the differences,
and imagination the similitudes of things.
—*Percy Bysshe Shelley*

Rights that do not flow
from duty well performed are not worth having.
—*Mathatma Gandhi*

Relatives are like flies to honey
when it comes to money.
—*R. R. Washington*

Reasonable joking decides great things.
—*Winston Churchill*

Reading makes a full man
—mediation a profound man
—discourse a clear man.
—*Benjamin Franklin*

Rules of my life include making
business a pleasure,
and pleasure my business.
—*Aaron Burr*

Ridiculing philosophy is really to philosophize.
—*Blaise Pascal*

Reading a good book
is like conversing with the noblest minds
of bygone ages.
—*Rene Descartes*

Reason is whole pleasure,
all the joys of sense lie in these three words
—Health, Peace, and Competence.
—*Alexander Pope*

Science

gives us knowledge,
but only philosophy
can give us wisdom.
—*Anonymous*

Sometimes life has to be lived using a fast-forward button.
—*Anonymous*

Sky is the daily bread for the eyes.
—*Ralph Waldo Emerson*

Some folks sometimes can be so busy doing nothin'
that they seem indispensable.
—*Abe Martin*

Saddest hour of a man's life is when
he tries to get money without earning it.
—*Horace Greeley*

Someone has said that character is what
a person does when nobody is looking.
—*Anonymous*

Success carries a strong sense of obligation.
—*Sigmund Freud*

Self-denial is simply a method
by which man arrests his progress.
—*Oscar Wilde*

So we may accomplish great things,
we should live as if we were never going to die.
—*Marquis de Vauvenargues*

Systems exercise the mind,
but faith enlightens and guides it.
—*Voltaire*

Sometimes your pleasure's a sin
and sometimes a sin's a pleasure.
—*Lord Byron*

Some folks never begin t' figure till ther's nothin' t' add.
—*Abe Martin*

Small service is true service.
—*Henry Wadsworth Longfellow*

The art of living
is more like that of wrestling
than of dancing. The main thing
is to stand firm and be ready
for an unforeseen attack.
—*Marcus Aurelius*

There are two things to aim at in life:
first, to get what you want and then to enjoy it.
Only the wisest ever achieve the second.
—*Logan Pearsall Smith*

Twice two makes four is an excellent thing,
but if we are to give everything its due,
twice two makes five is sometimes
a very charming thing too.
—*Fyodor Dostoevski*

To remain ignorant of what occurred
before you were born is to remain always childlike.
—*Cicero*

The more wit we have the more we want.
—*Anonymous*

To say the least, a city life
makes one more tolerant and liberal
in one's judgment of others.
—*Henry Wadsworth Longfellow*

There comes an hour of sadness with the setting sun,
Not for the sins committed, but the things not done.
—*Minot Judson Savage*

There's few things in this life
that equal th' sensation o' bein' paid up.
—*Abe Martin*

Tenacity is what makes the impossible possible,
the possible achievable, and the achievable work.
—*Anonymous*

There is nothing so stupid as an educated man,
if you get him off the thing he was educated in.
—*Will Rogers*

Talk is cheap or some folks would be broke all th' time.
—*Abe Martin*

The arrows of our anguish fly farther than we guess.
—*Rudyard Kipling*

Trouble with most people is that they think
with their hopes or fears
rather than with their minds.
—*Will Durant*

There's one thing we all ought t' let people find out fer 'emselves,
an' that's how honest we are.
—*Abe Martin*

The fixity of a habit is generally in direct proportion to its absurdity.
—*Marcel Proust*

The dignity of truth is lost with too much protesting.
—*Ben Jonson*

Time ripens all things. No man's born wise.
—*Miguel de Cervantes*

Trifles make up the complete happiness
or the total misery of everyday life.
—*Alexander Smith*

Two great talkers will not travel far together.
—*George Borrow*

The person who lets themselves be bored
is even more contemptible than the bore.
—*Samuel Butler*

The rough and rocky road is the path to true virtue.
—*Michael Eyquem de Montaigne*

The single greatest thing of living
is the gift of being personally able
to make the best of your life.
—*Anonymous*

Ther hain't nothin' as uncommon as common sense.
—*Abe Martin*

The sound of droning voices is the price we pay
so we may hear the music of our own opinions.
—*Anonymous*

Universe:
a place full of magical things
patiently waiting for
our wits to grow sharper.
—*Eden Phillpotts*

Variety is
the very spice of life
that gives it all its flavor
and excitement.
—*William Cowper*

What a man says drunk he has thought sober.
—*British proverb*

We often git the reputation fer bein' a grouch
by talkin' plainly t' th' wrong bore.
—*Abe Martin*

We have forty million reasons for failure,
but not a single excuse.
—*Rudyard Kipling*

We have no more right to happiness
without producing it
than to wealth without producing it.
—*George Bernard Shaw*

What do we live for if it is not to make life less difficult for each other!
—*George Eliot*

We lie loudest when we lie to ourselves.
—*Proverbs*

What is bought is often cheaper than a gift.
—*Portuguese saying*

We become civilized not in proportion
to our willingness to believe,
but in proportion to
our willingness to doubt.
—*H. L. Mencken*

Whosoever will be cured of ignorance, must confess the same.
—*Michel de Montaigne*

What a curious shift we make to escape thinking.
—*Herman Melville*

Whatever liberates our spirit without
giving us self-control is disastrous.
—*Johann von Goethe*

When you lose be a lovable loser!
—*Benjamin Franklin*

When in doubt, don't!
—*Proverbs*

eXpression
**from looks and not lips
is the soul reflected.**
—M'Donald Clarke

You can't depend on your eyes when your imagination is out of focus.
—*Mark Twain*

Yet now and then you of wit,
will condescend to take a bit!
—*Jonathan Swift*

Yearn for the impossible.
—*Johann von Goethe*

You who depart from your own honesty
For vulgar praise, does it too dearly buy.
—*Ben Jonson*

You can observe a lot just by watching.
—*Yogi Berra*

You have not converted a man
because you have silenced him.
—*John Morley*

You can fake being funny
but you can't fake being witty.
—*Anonymous*

Your eyes make the best pictures when they are shut.
—*Samuel Coleridge*

Your eyes are of no use
without observing power.
—*Latin proverb*

You can keep the gold and silver
but give us your wisdom.
—*Arabian proverb*

You cannot fly like an eagle
with the wings of a wren.
—*William Hudson*

Your pride of ancestry increases
in the ratio of distance.
—*George William Curtis*

You may delay, but time will not.
—*Benjamin Franklin*

laZy people

are always
looking
for something
to do and never finding it.
—*Marquis de Vauvenargues*

There may come a day
Which crowns Desire with gift,
and Art with truth,
and Love with bliss,
and Life with wiser youth!
—*Bayard Taylor*